KeVon Q. Pippens

# The

# King's

# Decrees

31 TRUTHS THAT UNVEIL HIS HEART
AND REVEALS YOUR IDENTITY

PIONEER PUBLISHING

# Endorsements

Brilliant. Simple. Revolutionary. In *The King's Decree*, KeVon Pippens conveys the message of the Gospel and the implications of the finished work of Christ with such impeccable simplicity that it really sticks! This is one of those books you keep with your Bible and Journal and give away to all your friends and family for Christmas and birthdays! It's time to break free from the complicated, religious gobbly-gook presented in most churches, and begin to live from a place of true union and communion with Christ! It's from this place of sonship, and the reality of being seated with Christ in heavenly places, that actually releases the sweet fragrance of heaven on earth through our lives. Meditate on, and marinate in, each decree of this book and watch your life transform. This is an endorsement I've been waiting to write!

*Eric Green, Co-founder & Overseer, Kingdom Life Institute*

Identity has been a common struggle amongst most Christian believers throughout the ages. We struggle with classicism, racism, sexism, and humanism to name a few. Who am I? Why do I do the things I do? What does this God want from me? Do I actually care what He wants from me? Do I qualify? All of these are good questions from any sane person who chooses to be a God-follower. In the midst of a pursuit and hunger, answers often come out of what seems like nowhere to these questions. The King's Decree is nothing less than an answer.

So much is expected from us as Christians and even more is expected of us who say we are called to ministry. This expectation often does not come with a guide or a foundation of principles to help us attain the expectation. In this skillful, pragmatic book of teachings you will find the theological foundation needed to achieve the height of success in your operation as a day-to-day Christian or global spiritual leader. These principles work for everyone. So whether you are trying to just be a nice person in the work place or leader of a ministry of ten thousand followers, this was written for you.

In these writings, which fit in with your greatest commentaries, you will find out that you belong, none of your personal works matter without Christ at the center, and with him at the center, there is not an end to what you can achieve for Him. In all honesty, many of the teachings and religious concepts that we possess cannot be found anywhere in the Holy Bible. This book sweeps in like a secret agent and dispels many Christian myths about our relationship with God perhaps without you even noticing. Take a look because you have thought inaccurately and related to your God incorrectly for too long!

My last statement is a phrase that I use in preaching all the time. After reading this book, "You can operate from a place that you have deserved to operate from all along!" Now The King's Decree can become Your Decree.

*Pastor Gerald Pace, Founder, The Sanctuary Movement, St. Louis, MO*

In The Kings Decrees, Pippens reveals God's decree of "It Is Finished" over everyone who calls Him Lord. This is certainly a fresh approach from this ancient portfolio of promises."

*Matt Wade, campus pastor, Cross Point Church, Nashville, TN*

In a day where we're constantly bombarded with negativity, circumstances, and situational concerns, it's always good to be reminded of the promises and declarations that can be found in the Holy Bible.

As an avid Bible reader and consummate lover of the profound allegory, metaphors, and revelatory jewels that are housed therein, I believe that *The King's Decrees* will greatly assist the believer in extrapolating fundamental truths daily. This is essential to the success and sustainability of the Christian walk. Proverbs 18:21 declares, "*Death and life are in the power of the tongue, And those who love it will eat its fruit.*" This powerful truth resonates throughout *The King's Decrees* , and I believe its contents will be divinely paramount in creating an unprecedented, unparalleled paradigm shift to anyone who will turn its pages.

*KeVon Pippens*, a man of great apostolic prophetic insight, wisdom and prayer, speaks as a true end-time oracle of God. His constant chase for the heart of the Father is evident in everything he sets forth to accomplish spiritually. The creditability and the validity of the anointing and glory that rests upon his life are surely manifested with each turn of the page of *The King's Decrees.* From the King's lips to the author's pen, to our hearts and ears, comes the consuming fire of God that will enlighten, empower, and equip any believer to aspire to become naturally supernatural.

A great man of faith and wisdom beyond his years, the high spiritual acumen of KeVon Pippens proves that he's surely no novice to spiritual and revelatory knowledge. It's also just as painfully obvious that KeVon has been granted "top secret" clearance in the Spirit whereby the hidden treasures of the Father are revealed, discovered, and obtained. What a joy and sheer delight that he thought it not robbery to share his findings with the Body of Christ and the world.

*The King's Decrees* is a must have in your library. It's an anointed arrow of the Lord's deliverance. Not only is this a book full of divine revelation, but it is also a great tool of spiritual weaponry, mandatory and imperative to possess in the spiritual arsenal of the believer.

***Michael Jenkins, Founder, Shekinah Deliverance Ministries, St. Louis, MO***

# CONTENTS

## Section 2: The Benediction

# Dedication

This book I'm dedicating to my beautiful wife Cedrica Pippens, my mom and grandma.

I am the most blessed man in the world. I have learned so much from these women. The love that is expressed through their lives are a constant inspiration to me, and reminder that life is about pouring out His love wherever you go. My prayer for them is that they will continually grow in their revelation of the love of God and continue to let the world see it.

Special love to everyone who has poured into my life and encouraged me to walk out my destiny. You mean more to me than I could ever express. I also want to send a special appreciation to anyone who has ever allowed me to serve your congregation. Last but not least, I dedicate this book to everyone who will ever read it. My prayer for you is that you may experience the Father's heart and grow in your identity as a child of God. Love you all!

# Section One:

# The King's Decrees

# Decree #1

# "Distance no longer exists between God and the believer"

*"Then behold the veil of the temple was torn from top to bottom..."*

*–Matt. 27:51*

---

From the beginning, the Father created man as relational beings. He has placed within us the innate desire to fellowship with others. It was His desire from the beginning to have unbroken fellowship with mankind. Upon the fall of Adam (Man), a veil was placed between man and God which caused man to become aware of their "nakedness" rather than their consciousness being set on the glory of God. In Eden God walked with mankind in the cool of the day, and there, communion with Him was the norm. There was no distance between them. They walked together in perfect harmony. This union that was lost at the Fall has been restored in the flesh (body) of Christ (Heb.10:19-20). We have been reunited to the Father in the Body of Jesus Christ. The Father sent his Son to remove the distance between God and man once and for all. The sin that separated man from God, Jesus became on the Cross, and the wrath that man deserved was poured out upon Him. "For God so loved the world that He gave His only begotten Son, that whosoever believes in Him should not perish but have everlasting life" (John 3:16). Eternal life is knowing Jesus. The Father gave Jesus to eternally restore relationship between Him and mankind. Our rejection of Him couldn't keep Him from loving us. There are many in the Body of Christ who teach that rituals, strivings, and great laboring bring us closer to Him, when in reality we have been made one in the Son. Jesus was the Father's gift to humanity, and humanity's hearts are their gift to Him.

# Decree #2

# "A lie left humanity in darkness, so the Father sent Truth to reveal our true identity"

*"Then God said, Let Us make man in Our image, and according to Our likeness..."*

*–Gen. 1:26*

---

The goal of satan is to convince man of a lie concerning their identity. In the garden he convinced Eve that by eating the fruit she would be made like God. When in truth, she was already made like God. He had made mankind in His image and likeness. She believed the lie and ate the fruit in hope of becoming something that she ALREADY was. Once you receive Jesus Christ as your Lord and Savior, you are made a new creation, righteous, and holy in Christ. The first Adam did nothing to earn his "image," and neither do we. He has given us His image as a gift, but the reality of what you manifest is hinged upon what you believe. We must take rest in what the Lord has said about us. We are no longer under the law (works based relationship) trying to prove ourselves to God. We can't impress Him, He is God, but we can enter into His desires. His desire is for us to enter into His rest. This rest is found in the reality of Who He is, and who He has created us to be. Take rest in this, that the Holy Spirit within you cries out through all eternity that you are a son (child) of God, and that He is producing sonship in you. The moment that you stop striving to be a son and believe the truth is the moment that you will find rest and assurance that you are His beloved. This rest doesn't equate to laziness, but a place of authority. Jesus rested while the disciples were panicking in the storm. He could do this because He knew who the Father made Him to be and from this place He effortlessly manifested heaven on earth. You are His child, and nothing can pluck you from His hands. That is the truth!

# Decree #3

## "The Cross was about more than cleaning up some sinners. It was about the Father's love revealing to man their true value."

*"What is man that You are mindful of Him..."*

*–Psalm 8:4*

---

For many the Cross is simply seen as a means of escaping the flames of hell. So often, people preach the Cross in a way that sends a message that Jesus came to clean us up so that we could have a chance at being loved by God. This is an improper view of the Cross. The truth is, Jesus was sent because of love, and by love to reveal to us our true identity. The Fall, which occurred because of faith in a lie, created a false image within humanity. The Father knew who He created man to be, but mankind had been seduced and influenced by the lie of satan. Jesus came as the prototype, the perfect example of who the Father had created us to be. He demonstrated what sonship looked like. He came as a man, living under the complete influence of the Holy Spirit. He came and gathered individuals (disciples) who had previously identified themselves through religion and their occupations and revealed to them their true identity. Great astonishment filled the hearts of the disciples as they saw who they were truly created to be. David asked the question, "What is man that you are mindful of him…?" Great joy comes when we find out that we are not the lie that satan has tried to convince us that we are. Just think about it, what value must the God who created the universe have for us to be so mindful of us. He could set all of His attention on creating new galaxies, stars, and heavens, yet we are at the center of His heart. The value of something is revealed in the price one is willing to pay for it. My friends, your value is not measured by society nor is it found in your great accomplishments. It's not found in the amount of money you acquire or the legacy you leave. Meditate upon this truth. The Father's value for you is Jesus Christ, the Only Begotten Son.

# Decree #4

## "The Finished Work of the Cross qualifies you to walk in sonship. You can't earn it, nor can you perform for it. Receive it through grace, by faith."

*"For it was fitting for Him, for whom are all things and by whom are all things, in bringing sons to glory..."*

*–Heb. 2:10*

---

"This only I want to learn from you: Did you receive the Spirit by the works of the law, or by the hearing of faith" (Gal. 3:2). Paul asks the Galatians this as a rhetorical question, because they had fallen from grace. The Galatians heard the message of grace, but like most of the Church, they inter-mingled it with the Law. Paul went on to shed light on this truth, "You entered into the family of God by grace (the Cross) through faith." So often when we get saved, we are told that we have to do all of these things in order to be loved and received by God. The truth is, you are His child, and there is nothing you can do that will ever cause Him not to love you. You don't earn the right to be a son, Jesus has taken care of that. You enter into relationship through the Finished Work of the Cross by faith. Faith is as simple as believing. Your works don't qualify you to be a son, nor do they impress the Father. There are far more important things like your heart. He is relationship driven not works driven. A revelation of relationship empowers you to work from a position of rest. Jesus restored us to our proper position with the Father. In the beginning man started off with God, left, and has received reconciliation through the flesh of Jesus Christ. The story of the Prodigal Son is a great representation of this truth. The son started off as royalty and had access to everything. He had been given the authority to steward and appropriate his inheritance from the Father, then he went off into the "world." After the world beat him up, the thought comes to him that he can return to his father's house. The world had trained him to be a slave, and being so he thought that he had to return to his original country (or kingdom) a slave. Something remarkable happens when He decides to return. The Father sees him from afar off, runs to him, and kisses him on the neck. In the mind of the son, the father would only receive him back as a slave. The reality was that the father never stopped loving the son for being a "bad" boy. He wasn't moved by his son's frivolous living. He loved him unconditionally. When he kissed him upon the neck it was a sign that he has been received back into the family. When we receive the kiss of the Cross we are immediately joined to the Head (The Father). The sobering reality is that most still feel as though they have to prove themselves to God. The Prodigal Son thought this very thought, even after the father had received him with great joy. The amazing thing we see in this story is that the father never brings up what his son did (past). He did the exact opposite by clothing him in his royal garments and affirming him in his identity as a son. Put off striving for His acceptance. You are accepted. Beloved, you are His child.

# Decree #5

# "You look just like your Daddy!"

*"So God created man in His own image, in the image of God He created him, both male and female"*

*–Gen. 1:27*

---

We live in a society that is filled with people seeking to "become." Most of their "becoming" is usually measured by how well they are keeping up with their peers, their level of intelligence, and striving to achieve more than everyone else. This mind-set causes hopelessness and low self image in the hearts of those who perceive themselves to be of less value than others around them, and in many cases causes them to even want to be those people. This is one of the reasons there is such a low display of creativity and uniqueness in society, because people don't embrace who they have been created to be. Lucifer had this same mentality before he was thrown from heaven. He was driven by pride and desired to be God. He wasn't content being who God designed him to be. Friends, I want to encourage you in this truth, "You are fearfully and wonderfully made." The Father was intentional in the way that He made you. You're not weird nor are you of less value than your brother or sister. When He made you, He looked upon you and said, "It is good." You are beautiful to the Father and you look just like Him. He made you in His image. You are an expression of what He looks like. We all look like Him, but are yet so intrinsically different. We are all a unique expression of the Father and He loves us all. There is no need to compete or attain to be your brother. We are one body and are valued the same in the heart of God. He has placed within you something that is designed to impact this world for the rest of time. I want to encourage you to rest in the truth that you are accepted by Him, and walk in the freedom of who He has created you to be as an individual. No longer be bound to the bondage of performing for acceptance. The revelation that you are accepted, empowers you to "perform" efficiently from a place of authority and authenticity. Rest in this truth, "You look just like your Daddy!" What's better than that?

# Decree #6

# "Eternal life is knowing God"

*"You search the Scriptures, for in them you think you have eternal life; and these are they that testify of Me"*

*–John 5:39*

From the beginning of time, God has always been a relational God. His desire has always been to have a close relationship with His creation. So often in our pursuit to "know" God, we never actually go to Him. The Pharisees were searching for eternal life with God in scrolls, when the Messiah was walking right among them. The "way" to the Father was in their midst, but in the midst of seeking for Him in a book, they failed to receive the revelation that He desired to commune directly with them. Eternal life is not the knowledge of every scripture in the Bible; it's about knowing

Him. Scripture is true and informs you about truth, but Truth is a person. His name is Jesus. So often, the possibility of knowing Him is put off as a future event when we cross on over into that "sweet by and by," when the truth is He has placed eternity in our hearts. He has filled us with Holy Spirit and has made us His secret place. Don't settle for simply reading about Him, when you have been reconciled to "know" Him. Jesus modeled what it looked like to walk in communion with the Father. The disciples recognized that the key to the life Jesus lived was found in His relationship with the Father. They never asked Him how to work miracles, how to raise the dead, or how to cast out a devil. They inquired, "Lord, Teach us how to pray." In essence, the disciples were asking, "Lord, teach us how to walk in intimacy." Prayer is not about how loud and hard you can scream for God to be pleased with you (not saying that there is anything wrong with loud praying). It is about growing in intimacy with God, and living out of that place in the world. Everything that Jesus did among men came with ease because it flowed from a walk of communion with the Father. He drew near to the Father. When we draw to Him, He draws to us (James 4:8). This is not talking about distance but revelation. A person can sit next to an individual in class every day of the year and never know anything about that person because they never reached out to initiate the development of a relationship. This scenario is true as it pertains to knowing God as it is seen with the Pharisees. He walked among them but they were clueless as to who He was. Friends, He has invited you to the banqueting table of His presence and is waiting to feast with you in the glory. Never settle for knowledge when you have been invited to know Him eternally.

# Decree #7

# "You life is not wrapped up in your past, it is wrapped up and hidden in Christ"

*"For you died, and your life is hidden with Christ in God"*

*–Col. 3:3*

Glory to God for the great exchange that occurred on the Cross! Praises be unto Him for causing us to triumph over every obstacle and device that once defined us! You are a new creation in Christ Jesus, and His blood has disarmed every demonic power in your life. This is the truth friends. He came, defeated the devil, ascended and took captive all captivity. Satan seeks to keep believers ignorant to this truth, thus causing them to repeat cycles of frustration and disappointment. Many have received salvation, but still walk through life answering to their past. Beloved the truth is that what defined you before you came to Christ has been buried. The "nature" that plagued you and caused you distress has been put to death in the body of Jesus. Let this truth set in, "The person you are now has never existed before." The old has passed away, behold all things have become new. He has taken everything that represented the fall and placed it in a grave forever, and what Satan desires to do is use your past as a weapon to rob you of your present. A disarmed enemy is holding a gun that no longer has the power to kill you, because your life has been hidden in the body of the Almighty God. God is not holding what you did yesterday against you. Shame is no longer your portion. He took on the shame to release you into a place of freedom. Truth came to defeat the lie that seeks to keep you timid in your relationship with the Lord. Someone reading this book is struggling with the truth that God accepts you and that He is happy with you. Leave those grave clothes in the grave! In other words, let the dead bury the dead! He has positioned you to reign as a child who is now identified by what Christ has done. He has forgotten your past and is anticipating the manifestation of your future. Leave your past in the grave, and go forth in resurrection power! You have been raised in the father's glory, and restored in His image.

*Prayer:*

*Father, I thank You for Your unfailing, everlasting, and unconditional love for me. You love me so much that You sent Jesus to die in my place while I was yet an enemy against You. Your goodness is unsearchable and I am full of thanksgiving for Your kindness towards me. I thank you for erasing my past and ordaining my future. I thank you that my life is hidden in you and that my past has been disarmed from binding me any longer. The blood of Jesus has freed me from the law of sin and death and launched me into a life characterized by grace, freedom, and truth. I receive what Jesus has done on the Cross and boldly declare that I shall never allow my past to define me again. I am a new creation and the new me has never existed before. I decree that my life is established upon Truth and that I have been set free. I seal this prayer and enter into this reality, in the name of Jesus. Amen.*

# Decree #8

# "Forgive for love's sake"

*"Freely you have received; freely give"*

*–Matthew 10:8*

---

"But you don't know what they did to me."

"You don't know what they said about me."

"I'll forgive, but I refuse to forget."

"I've got too much pride to give them the satisfaction of being forgiven."

There is this virus that has infected so many people around the world and throughout history. Its name is un-forgiveness. It is this very thing that has severed marriages, destroyed families, and altered destinies. At some point we have all encountered pain from the actions of another individual, but our response has always been up to us. Have you ever stopped to ask yourself the question, "Why haven't I forgiven this person?" Yes it hurt, but it also hurts when you hit your funny bone, yet you are so forgiving of that piece of furniture that caused you the pain. Why is this? What causes us to be so resistant to forgive one another? My friends, the answer to this question is pride. It is the thought that another individual is not worthy of our forgiveness. Jesus told the disciples to freely give what had been given to them. That word applies to the area of forgiveness. As we grow in revelation of what it means to walk as children of God, we find that being quick to forgive is something we have been called to be. Stephen was in the process of being stoned to death, yet he was full of compassion and forgiveness. Stephen had a revelation of love that caused him to respond in forgiveness while being murdered. Love is a person as well as Forgiveness. His name is Jesus. While we were enemies against God, he sent His son because He is love. Yes, we were warring against Him, but His love is unstoppable. Love didn't see us as enemies, it saw our need. We needed forgiveness. So often, people say, "You need to forgive for yourself. It's not about them, it's about you." That root of that statement is pride. Yes forgiving blesses you, but that is not true forgiveness. God didn't forgive us because He needed to. He forgave because He is love, and we needed to be reconciled. Forgiveness releases the ministry of reconciliation.

Forgiveness that is driven by selfishness doesn't restore, it reinforces independence. We weren't created to be independent, but to depend; first to depend on God, and to empower each other as a family. When the revelation of the beauty of forgiveness is enlightened within your heart, it changes the way you perceive people. You are no longer as moved by their "bad behavior," as you are God's immense love for them. This is not some fairy tale; this is the reality of being possessed by love. His love changes everything. If you have been hurt, I want to encourage you to take time to perceive them through the eyes of Jesus. Let the ministry of the Cross; the ministry of reconciliation minister to your heart. What ever happened, place it in the hands of Jesus. Cast your cares upon Him, and get under the streams of His raging love. Your neighbor needs you. Offense blinds you from seeing their value and need for love. I encourage you to forgive for love's sake!

# Decree #9

# "Don't lot man the authority to choose when you love."

*"But God demonstrates His own love towards us, in that while we were still sinners, Christ died for us."*

*–Romans 5:8*

---

We are living in a time where there is an overwhelming sense of entitlement that exists within the hearts of men. It is this attitude that causes man to feel as though someone owes them something. This attitude is one that is driven by pride. As we examine the life of Jesus we never see this attitude of entitlement. If you expect anyone to feel entitled to something you would think it would be Jesus. For goodness sake, He's only the Messiah, but His attitude is the complete opposite. Jesus left His throne and came to earth as one-hundred percent man, and lived one-hundred percent under the influence of God. He didn't come saying, "I am the anointed One and you better respect Me." Rather He came and humbled Himself to love. Throughout all of the Gospels there are countless accounts of individuals dishonoring Jesus, yet in the midst of it all He remained unmoved. What caused Him to do this? Friends the answer is love. The entire reason for which He had been sent was inspired and motivated by love. People slandered His name, spat in His face, snatched hair from His beard, beat Him, lied on Him, and yet He was only moved by love. He was so compelled by love that those very people who were seeking to hurt Him, were the joy set before Him as He went to endure the Cross. It was still His pleasure to die for those very people, because His life was governed by love. Love isn't just something that we don when it's convenient. It's more than serving the homeless, a hug, and a smile. It's the power of seeing through the eyes of the Father. He sees through all of mans "bad behavior" and sees the beautiful creation he spoke into existence. He sees their potential, their value, and purpose. When He looks at them, He sees past what they are doing, and sees their need. This love is not something that can be conjured up. It begins with receiving love. The more we receive the Father's love, the more we love others. The Cross is a perfect picture of His love. Picture a cross, it has a vertical beam and an horizontal beam. Love has to first occur vertically, man receiving God's love, and loving Him back. Then, after love has occurred vertically, it empowers the us to pour His love out horizontally. It is this love that empowers you to authentically manifest the Kingdom in the earth. Love is the way every time friends! Let this love govern your heart and transform the world around you!

# Decree #10

# "You are His fragrance in the world"

*"For we are the fragrance of Christ among those who are being saved and among those who are perishing"*

*–2 Cor. 2:15*

---

You are the fragrance of Christ. I remember reading this and thinking, "What in the world does that mean?" What does it mean to be His fragrance? When studying the lifestyle of Jesus and examining His walk in the earth, we find that Jesus was fragrance of the Father. Everywhere He went, He diffused His Fathers "fragrance." When I think of a fragrance, I think of an atmosphere. The fragrance of something embodies characteristics of that thing. The fragrance of cinnamon smells sweet yet herby all at once. Its fragrance embodies its taste. As Christ's fragrance, we diffuse Him everywhere we go. We carry the very climate of heaven everywhere we go. Jesus, being the fragrance of the Father, would enter a city and it would be completely rocked. Multitudes of people would follow Him, everyone would be healed, devils cast out, and the dead were being raised. Jesus did what He saw the Father doing, and diffused His fragrance in every place. We have the awesome privilege of being the fragrance of Christ to those who are being saved and to those who are perishing (that they might be saved). Now you are probably asking the question, "How do I diffuse this fragrance?" Just "be." You are already His fragrance. The fruit of being His fragrance manifests when we get a revelation that we are His fragrance and embody Him. We are His body, it's no longer us, but it is Christ living in and through us. Revelation of this truth causes us to walk with a greater awareness of His presence, which results in us diffusing heaven everywhere we go. Being His fragrance means that you diffuse healing, miracles, deliverance, and power! This revelation empowers not to strive to be His fragrance, but to accept that you all ready are. You have been empowered to simple "be." As a child of God, like Christ, you carry the reality of the kingdom within you in the form of a person. His name is The Holy Spirit, or the spirit of the Lord. He is the very climate of heaven, and you are His temple. You are no longer bound to atmospheres or heavy climates, because the climate you carry is superior to all others. Rest in this truth and release Him in every place. The more you embrace this truth, the greater its impact will be on those around you. Remember, you are the thermostat and the climate shifter. Go forth and diffuse His fragrance in all the world!

# Decree #11

# "Slipping into a muddy puddle does not make you the dirt you fell in"

*"She said, "No one, Lord." And Jesus said to her, "Neither do I condemn you; go and sin no more.""*

*–John 8:10*

Falling into dirt doesn't make you dirt. So often, man's attention is focused on who you're not, instead of who you are. Satan and people are the only ones who brings up your past to condemn you. God never uses your past to condemn you, because the truth is, you are not defined by your past. The woman who was living an adulterous lifestyle had people around her who decided that she needed to die for her actions, but Jesus exposing the heart of the Father, declared that she not be condemned. He told her to, "Go and sin no more." What Jesus was talking about here wasn't behavior modification. He was declaring a new identity over her. He was calling her out of the "mud," and releasing her into a new identity. This is proven in the following verse when He says, "I am the light of the world. He who follows me shall not walk in darkness, but shall have the light of life" (John 8:11). Those who are in Christ are no longer identified by nor bound to an identity governed by darkness. He has given us an element that is always superior to darkness. It's called light. Jesus completed this work on the cross. The Father made Jesus who knew no sin to become sin on a Cross for us (2 Cor. 5:21). Jesus didn't become the action of sin on the Cross, He embodied the sin nature. This was the great exchange. He became what we were, so that we could become what He is. You are not who you were before you met Christ. When you received Him as your Savior, your old man was placed in the grave and you received a new nature. You have been made a new. Condemnation is no longer your portion. God does not use your past to condemn you, even if it was a few moments ago. In the Body of Jesus, the Father has extended an eternal plumb line of forgiveness to those who will receive. That wrath that man so often desires to unleash upon you was poured out upon Christ on the Cross. If you find yourself acting in a way that doesn't agree with your new nature, don't fall from grace. Instead of falling from Grace, fall into it. Grace empowers you to live above and in dominion over your old nature and to manifest sonship in Christ. Grace empowers you as the righteousness of God in Christ Jesus. This is a new and living way my friends! Rest in this truth, "You're not who you used to be, and Holy Spirit is about to reveal to you that you are more than you ever thought you could be."

# Decree #12

# "The greatest weapon of resistance is submission"

*"In all your ways acknowledge Him, and He shall direct your paths"*

*–Prov. 3:6*

---

So often right after getting saved, and even for individuals who have been saved a while, the question arises, "Why am I still being tempted, and how do I resist the devil?" The most popular responses are, "Go on a fast and kill your flesh," "Brother, you've just got to fight the devil," or "War in the spirit until he leaves you alone." While these are all sincere answers, they are all driven by our own efforts and strength. I believe there is a more proficient way of doing this and it doesn't require my sweat and hard efforts. It's called gazing upon the Lord. There are several things that occur as we gaze upon the Lord. We behold His beauty and experience His holiness. We grow in revelation of who He is, and by doing so we grow in revelation about who we are. Once receiving a revelation of who we are in Him, we are no longer moved by the enemy which in turn causes us to "sweatlessly" resist Him. I believe for so many, they experience this constant battle of trying to resist the demonic because they spend all of their efforts engaging it and being attentive to it. It's so much more effective to take those efforts being used to engage the devil, and gaze upon Jesus. Jesus modeled for us how to resist the devil. Jesus walked in constant communion with the Father and received the Father's revelation. When approached by the devil himself on the mountain, Jesus never flinches. There is no wrestling occurring nor is there great warfare. Jesus was only moved by what He believed, and what He believed was shaped from the time He spent with the Father. The devil had nothing in Christ, and there was nothing he could do to impress Him. When we constantly keep the Lord before us, acknowledging Him in every way, it changes the way we see things. It empowers us to see from heaven to earth. It enlightens us and causes us to see from His perspective. It empowers us to perceive from a seat of victory. We have been made to sit in heavenly places in Christ Jesus. If we are seated in heavenly places in Christ, that means we are in a superior position above the demonic. We have been endowed with authority over all of the power of the enemy and have been empowered to trample on him. The demonstration of this authority becomes active as we grow in relationship, because as we grow in relationship, we grow in revelation of who we are. This is the power of keeping our gaze upon the Lord. Rest in this truth; "You are seated in heavenly places in Christ Jesus, and He has positioned you to reign in sweatless victory!"

# Decree #13

# "Your mind was made for heaven."

*"Set your mind on things above, not on things on earth..."*

*–Col. 3:2*

---

As sons and daughters of a supernatural Father, we have been made to live naturally supernatural. For many, being supernatural is a goal many are seeking to attain, but in truth as born again believers, we have already been made supernatural. The conflict is not with the finished works of the Cross, it's with our belief system. What we hold to be true in our hearts is what steers our minds and determines the position from which we perceive. Being that we are seated in heavenly places in Christ Jesus (Eph.2:6), it is only right that we think from that position. We must first believe that we are seated in that place with Christ. Most still believe the thought that they are gross and awful human beings who aren't worthy to be in the

Presence of a holy God. I've got good news friends; He thinks you are worthy. The awesome truth is that you didn't even have to qualify yourself, He sent Jesus to take care of that for you. It's called the blood, the ministry of reconciliation. He has removed all distance between us, and seated us with Him, in Jesus Christ. Before we can began thinking from a heavenly perspective, we must first believe that we are seated there. The Bible has informed us, "As a man thinks in his heart, so is he" (Prov. 27:3). The thoughts that began in the mind, and were accepted as truth in the heart, become a benchmark from which we measure all further information. This being so, it is important that we capture and believe truth. This brings me to this decree. The Father designed our minds for heaven. We have been made to perceive from heaven's perspective; which in tern causes what we believe to be based on heaven's perspective and not what is earthly. What we believe is also what becomes our conviction, and truth upon which we stand. Heaven-set minds are a gateway for the Kingdom to be released on earth. When heaven's truth is our conviction, we are no longer impressed by sickness, depression, and poverty. It causes us to see through the lenses of heaven's reality. There is no sickness, poverty, or depression in heaven. Jesus perceived from this realm. He walked with His head in heaven, and His feet on the earth. That's why He encountered what would seem to be the worst cases, yet be unmoved. This is so because He saw through the lenses of another reality. Regardless of what He encountered, He overcame it with sweatless victory. He has designed us to perceive from that same reality. Man would have us to think that we are limited to what is occurring around us, but we sit in a realm that is superior to this one. There is a phrase out there that says, "You are so heavenly minded, that you are no earthly good." That couldn't be further from the truth. The more heavenly minded we become, the more earthly good we are. There are ideas, inventions, and treasures that will only be birthed in the earth by people who see from heaven's view. Rest in this truth, "Your mind was made to see through eternity."

# Decree #14

# "Your life is a melody before the Lord"

*"...Present your bodies a living sacrifice..."*

*–Romans 12:1*

So often when we think of a sacrifice, the thought of slaying bulls, goats, and birds comes to mind. It often illustrates a gory image in our minds, instead of one of beauty. More often than not, Roman 12:1 is equated to some task of great laboring and "killing" of your flesh. Here Paul is not instructing the people to have a flesh slaying party; he is encouraging them in their identity. In other words, "You're not who you used to be, this is who your are! Receive this reality and walk in it!" In our studying of the Bible, sacrifice is always equated to an act of worship. Presenting our bodies as a living sacrifice, is presenting our bodies as an active instrument of worship to the Lord. As an active instrument of worship, our life plays a melody that is unique to us as individuals, and one that is recognized in the heart of the Father. Worship extends and is not limited to singing in a building. We have this awesome opportunity to walk with the Holy Spirit as He leads us in the heavenly dance. We hear the melody that He places in our hearts and it comes forth as a sweet smelling savor before the King. So often, we become distracted by someone's dance and miss out on the melody He wants to release through us. Many times we are so convinced that what is happening in someone else's life is so wonderful, to the point that it causes us to devalue our own beauty. The amazing truth about God is that He is not more interested in one individual than He is another. His heart is to see each one of us walking in the fullness of what He has designed us to be, with full confidence in what He has done. Your song is just as much important as your brother's. The tune of this melody is beautified and perfectly tuned in the place of rest and submission. The freedom of sound flows as we allow Him to lead (direct) this dance called like. As He leads the orchestra of our affairs it plays out as the masterpiece that He dreamed before we were ever created. He knew you and called you into existence intentionally. The world needs to hear your song. There is a sound that your life has been marked to release in the earth. Never underestimate your existence. Your being is not a mistake. You've been adorned with beauty that goes beyond anything you could imagine. Rest in Him, and let your melody be heard!

# Decree #15

# "What He is doing in you is greater than what is happening around you"

*"...He who is in you is greater than he who is in the world..."*

*−1 John 4:4*

---

You are Jesus walking the earth. It is no longer you who lives, but this life you now live is governed by faith in the One who lives within you. He has defeated the world and has led you in a fixed triumph over the evil one who seeks to inflict havoc in the world. You are not a prisoner of circumstance. The enemy works in the business of magnification. He presents situations with the intent of magnifying them in your mind to distract you from the authority you have to speak to them. You see my friends, there is nothing that occurs around you that He won't provide to you the power to escape and overcome. The Jesus who lives within you is not afflicted, worried, nor is He the Jesus hanging on a cross. He is the resurrected Jesus who has overcome the world and now sits at the right hand of the Father. You are as victorious as Jesus Christ himself. Satan is the embodiment of evil, and all evil that exists in the world comes from him. It is his desire to use this evil to steal, kill, and destroy mankind. It is his desire to advance his kingdom as much as possible before the return of Jesus. I've got bad news for the devil! Jesus has already come back in the Body of His church. The Church is His body walking the earth. We are the embodiment of the One who is superior over every demonic system that exists. There is no obstacle, no sickness, nor is there any demonic force that has the power to overthrow the power He had legalized you to use. The reality of this truth bears fruit in our lives as we began to believe all that He has said about us. The grace that has come to us through the Cross serves as our supernatural enforcement that enables us to live in a constant state of rest in sonship and dominion over evil. Our awareness of this identity increases as we accept that we are the righteousness of God and that we are furiously loved by Him. Friends, my challenge to you is to remain impressed by His goodness and truth. This keeps your eyes attentive to what heaven is doing and positions you to receive His initiative for kingdom enforcement and advancement. You have been born to reign! Rest in this truth; "No weapon formed against you is greater than He that is within you!"

# Decree #16

**"Striving to live holy is birthed from a performance (Law) based mentality. He has made you holy, and you bear this fruit by relying upon the instruction of Grace."**

*"For the grace of God that brings salvation has appeared to all men, teaching us that, denying ungodliness and worldly lusts, we should live soberly, righteously, and godly in this present age"*

*–Titus 2:11-12*

Let's make this clear from the beginning in order that I might clearly elaborate on this truth; "You can't make yourself holy, no matter how hard you try!" Now take a deep breath, and exhale all that pressure you've carried to perform. Lay down your "props" and put on Christ. In Him there is rest to simply "be." For so long as a body we have been taught an "ABC" formula to living right and the "Seven Steps to Holiness." Preachers have presented a lists of rules that no one can live up to and has left many in despair feeling like God is angry with them because they couldn't become holy enough. Brothers and sisters, I've got Good News for you! Christ has made us holy (Heb.10:10). He became sin (it's entire nature) who knew no sin to make us righteous, holy, and blameless before the Father. Jesus gets the glory for this! We are holy, and He gets the glory! When we try to perform our way into holiness, we then begin to throw in the faces of others all that we have done to obtain what we believe to be a certain level of holiness. My friends, there are no levels to this, holy is holy. It's who you are. It's been imputed into your identity as a child of God. You look like your Daddy and have received His DNA. You have this great opportunity to REST. Accept what He has said about you! Only Believe! The Father didn't send Jesus so that you could go through a repetitive cycle of failure, frustration and defeat. He sent Him to reveal to you, your true identity. Those who believe on what He has said will produce the kingdom and continuously flow like a river in sonship. Throw away the lie that God is not happy with you and that you're not good enough. Your value is not in your performance, it's Jesus. Holiness identifies you as special, set apart, and precious. Jesus revealed to you that this is who you were when He died for you, and He has supplied you with Grace as a supernatural instructor and tour guide into deeper depths of your identity. You are no longer identified as a "sinner," you are a saint! You are no longer seen as a mistake, but a child of promise. Rest in this truth; "He became who you were to unveil who you were always created to be!"

# Decree #17

# "Your life is not defined by disappointments, it's defined by truth"

*"...Then you shall know the truth, and the truth shall set you free..."*

*–John 8:32*

---

A disappointment is not an indication that you aren't good enough; it is an indication that there is more. Never again allow disappointment to altar what you believe about yourself. Your greatness is not measured by circumstances; it is measured by the person of Jesus Christ. If you are in the earth as He is in heaven, then that is an indication that your greatness goes beyond that which is earthly. Any time you measure who you are by what is experienced in the earthly realm, you undermine your potential to fruitfully and efficiently blossom into all that you have been created to be. Jesus displayed to mankind the proper way to respond to unfortunate outcomes. His solution was faith. What happened on earth didn't move the conviction He had about what was occurring in heaven. His life wasn't measured by what occurred in the earth, it was measured, directed, and governed by what the Father was doing in heaven. When wine ran low He performed a creative miracle, when food was near depletion He multiplied it, and when approached by the sick He healed them. In every situation His life was established on truth. Truth is not what you see with the naked eye, it exists in another realm. Truth exists in the unseen and stands forever. One day the earth's grass will whither and fall away, yet His word will never whither. His word is forever established in heaven (the invisible/eternal realm). Jesus was only moved by what the Father had to say, and what appeared before Him was irrelevant. Disappointment is ineffective and unfruitful in the life of one who walks by faith. Walking by faith requires you to see from the Father's perspective. It sees from the eternal to time. It is anchored in the realm of truth. When what we believe is founded upon anything less than Truth, we position ourselves to experience identity theft, deception, and confusion. Jesus said to us (John 8:31) that when we abide in His word that we abide in truth. A key to continually moving in momentous success is resting in His word (both written and rhema). This means studying what has been written, hearing what is being spoken, and believing. Smith Wigglesworth declared, " I am only moved by what I believe." Friends, this is the truth for us all. Jesus has invited and empowered us to walk in continual reliance and dependence upon Him (Truth). He came and restored our identity and has made us overcomers! Remember, your greatness is not measured by what you are currently experiencing, but by the person of Jesus Christ. Now go forth and tap into your unlimited potential!

# Decree #18

## "DNA = Divine Nature Applied"

*"...And He sent them to preach the kingdom of God and to heal the sick..."*

*–Luke 9:2*

---

DNA encodes the genetic instructions that are used in determining our development and functioning. When we are first born, we carry the combined DNA of our earthly parents. This evidence is seen in how much we not only physically favor them, our future health, and even down to our personality. This is why often parents can see themselves in their children. When we are born again we receive the DNA of our Heavenly Father. Our entire make-up is altered, and the way in which we function changes. At one time, genetically, we only related to things by earthly principles, but now that we have been born again, our DNA is instructed and influenced by heaven. We are in the world, but not of it. As born again believers, we are endowed with authority and power (Luke 9:1) to do what we previously couldn't. We have exchanged our old nature for His divine nature. On the Cross Jesus became sin (our old nature and everything that came as a result of the Fall) in order that we might receive of His nature. It was the great exchange! With this exchange comes a new norm. Previously it was normal to be sick, to be emotionally unpredictable, and bound in unhealthy behavioral patterns. Our new norm is perfect health, joy like a river, and freedom to BE! His divine nature has been applied to everything we are. So often we are taught to labor and work for God to get these things, when the truth of the matter is that He has already worked it out for us. All we are instructed to do is receive. Not only has His divine nature been applied to us, but He has given us authority to apply His divine nature in the world around us. Jesus told the disciples to go and heal the sick, or in other words, to apply His divine nature to every body that didn't agree with heaven's environment. As His children who carry His DNA, we look like Him and naturally manifest Him in the earth. As you are reading this book, the currents of heaven's power is flowing through your body. You have been charged with His electricity and are powerful by nature. Previously we were powerless before the devil, but now we are positioned in a seat higher than he and daily bruise his head. Lay down the lie that you are still bound by an old nature. The old man has been buried, and you have been raised up by the glory of the Father. Now that's Good News!

# Decree #19

# "I made you for My Presence"

*"...Pray without ceasing..."*

*–1 Thessalonians 5:17*

---

You have been made to experience the Presence of God without ceasing. So often we think that we have to come in and out of His presence, when He has torn the veil to abide with us there permanently. The truth is, yes we have as secret place with God, but He also has a secret place within us. We are His secret place. We have the greatest hiding place that has ever existed; it's in Christ. We grow in the revelation of this truth through continual prayer. When you hear the words "continual prayer," I'm sure sweat bubbles appear on your forehead as you think about the hard work that has so often been associated with prayer. Prayer is more than speaking. Prayer is intentional attentiveness to God. Words aren't always involved. It's the awareness of having perfect unity with the Father and resting in the truth that nothing can pluck you out of His hands. From the beginning, His presence is where we always belonged. The Fall brought separation, but Jesus has restored unity. The ripping of Christ's body was the ripping of the veil that removed all distance between you and God once and for all. You have been made one, and your life is hidden in Him. Knowing this empowers you to walk in unbroken communion with Him all day long. It is this truth that positions you to live in dominion and not be a victim of life.

So often, in our constant strivings to become ready for His presence, we enter into a place of unhealthy despair. We often battle with whether or not we are worthy to even enter into His presence. My friends, you were made for it! He doesn't see you through eyes of condemnation, He sees you through eyes of love. Christ has qualified you to rest and reign in the glory realm. God is not holding out on you! You can have as much of Him as you desire. Something amazing happens as we pray without religious strongholds governing it. We find out how deep in the heart of Jesus we really are. Intimacy is always the first priority of prayer. It is His desire to take you into a deeper revelation of His love for you. It's the place where He reveals to you how He sees you, and shows you who you've been all along in Him. Praying without ceasing isn't so bad after all!

It's not another "lap" you have to run to prove that you are a "good" Christian to God. It's a place of bliss where you see Him and from that place you make Him known. You were made for this!

# Decree #20

# "You were made for My voice."

*"My sheep hear My voice, and I know them, and they follow Me."*

*–John 10:27*

---

      Powerful, majestic, and full of passion; It's the voice of God. He speaks to us, He knows us, and with love He compels us to follow Him. What an astonishing thought, the God of the universe, the creator of heaven and earth, the eternal God Himself knows and speaks to us. He takes pleasure in speaking to His children. With His voice He leads us in truth and draws us into Himself. He delights in sharing the mysteries of the Kingdom and the secrets of heaven with us. He is pleased to give us insight and strategies that empower us to fulfill our destiny. So often, because of a poor self-image, people enter into condemnation where they don't desire to hear His voice. Quite often, some would much rather have someone else hear God for them. And let's not forget the group of people that find it ludicrous to even consider that God still speaks to man. Beloved, what kind of father wouldn't speak to their children. He has more to say to us than we are willing to listen to. He wants to converse with us exceedingly more than we could ever desire to converse with Him.

Something unique about His voice is that it is multi-faceted. It is not one dimensional in the way that it is produced. His voice is not limited to our native language. He speaks in various forms, which includes but are not limited to the still small voice, audibly, trances, visions, dreams, impressions, our senses, miracles, signs, wonders, and the angelic. What an expression of His greatness and creativity! So many strive and feel like they have to fulfill a list of laws before they can hear the voice of God. So often in the midst of striving with good intentions, we miss the Voice. Friends, I want to invite you to "be still and know" that He is God. In the place of stillness there is rest, and in the rest you come to know that He is! In this place, your ears become sensitized to His voice that has been speaking to you all along. You don't have to work something up to hear His voice. You can simply ask Him, "Lord what are You saying?" "Lord what are you doing?" Always remember, "His yoke is easy." If it's overcomplicated, it's probably not Grace. It's by Grace that you are lead by His voice and have the awesome opportunity speak to and hear Him all day long. Walking with Him in this way not only allows us to experience the blessing of being with Him, but it equips us to effectively hear and share Him with those around us. As you embark upon this journey of communion, believe this truth, "You are His child, and you hear His voice."

# Decree #21

# "On your darkest day, He never loses sight of who you were created to be."

*"...Arise and eat..."*

*–1 Kings 19:5*

---

In 1 Kings 19, we see the great Prophet Elijah hiding in a cave from Jezebel. This is a side of Elijah that we don't see anywhere else in the Bible. In every other place Elijah displays great confidence and strength. Here, we see him in a dark place, pleading for God to take his life. Elijah exclaims, "It is enough! Now, Lord, take my life, for I am no better than my fathers!" There are occasions when we as people encounter situations where we might feel as though we have been backed into a corner, and they only way out is death. We see this lie spreading as suicides are becoming increasingly common as the solution of choice. Here we see

Jezebel is seeking to kill Elijah and him feeling his best option is to give up. We all have an enemy that is seeking to kill, steal, and destroy us. For you, it might not be Jezebel, but it might be depression, fear, or anxiety. Regardless of what it might be, the truth is, that those things don't have dominion over us. They aren't even legally ours to claim. He is our portion!

The enemy seeks to push you into a dark place as a tactic to highjack your mind. He wants to be magnified in your thoughts and to fill them with gross darkness. Elijah who had previously overturned darkness forgot who he was. When God responded to Elijah, He never once acknowledged what Jezebel was doing. He simple said to Elijah through an angel, "Arise and eat." Elijah thought that he was alone, and had to do it all himself. God wanted to remind him that He was with him. On Elijah's darkest day, God never lost sight who He created Elijah to be, or what He called him to do. One moment is not powerful enough to obliterate your destiny. Had that been so, Elijah would have died in the cave. Be encouraged, the Lord is with you. You are not in this alone. You have a companion that walks with you daily. His name is Holy Spirit. He will lead you into all truth concerning your identity, your purpose, and destiny. Arise and eat! Rise up in your identity, and eat of His truth. You are a mighty warrior, armed with power, and legalized by the Father to use it! I declare over your life that you will no longer experience victimization by the hands of the enemy, but that your living would bring terror upon the kingdom of darkness. Your victory was fixed over two thousand years ago! Go forth in faith knowing this, "If God be for you, then who can be against you!"

# Decree #22

# "You've been authorized to execute power."

*"Heal the sick, cleanse the lepers, raise the dead, cast out demons. Freely you have received, freely give."*

*—Matthew 10:8*

---

As a born again believer, it is your birthright to walk in the supernatural. It is not something that you earn; you have freely been allotted this inheritance. So many people forfeit this portion of their divine inheritance and regard it as something of the past. You have been designed to operate in the miraculous. As a child of God, it was always supposed to be your norm. So often, in the Body of Christ, there is this mindset that only "special" people are gifted to move in the miraculous. This mindset causes bodies of people to flock to names and causes them not to tap into their supernatural inheritance. Jesus informed us that these supernatural signs follow those who BELIEVE as a sign that points to the greatness and goodness of God.

The miraculous has in past times been something that has been over mystified and complicated by those who claim to have the special "goods" that the rest of us aren't fit to carry. The truth of the matter is, it is all about love. He calls us to demonstrate this power because it further exposes His glory and love for people. He has given us a kingdom asset called faith, which is used to generate these signs. So often we equate the working of faith to great feats of striving and hard work. This is why you will see people yelling at people during prayer and the casting out of devils. This is so because so often we forget the main element that is needed to produce the miraculous, it's called love. Love generates, forms, and gives expression to faith (Gal. 5:6). Love expresses the Father's heart so see humanity walking in wholeness and their original design. Through His eyes of love, you will come to the realization that we were never created to walk in sickness, depression, or poverty. We weren't designed to be subdued nor controlled by the elements of this world. In the beginning, God gave mankind dominion over every kingdom except His. Upon the Fall, satan gained authority, but Jesus came, took the keys back and has given them to the Church. We are now carriers of heaven's government and ambassadors sent forth to partner with our Father in causing His kingdom to be increased in the world. We do this by walking in the Spirit and living by faith. Faith is a kingdom asset that He has given us. It is up to us how we leverage it. You have therefore been authorized and deputized to carry and demonstrate the power of your Father. Remember this truth, "As He is, so are we in this world" (1 John 4:17).

# Decree #23

# "I've designed you for the deep."

*"It's the glory of God to conceal a matter, but the glory of kings is to search out a matter."*

*–Prov. 25:2*

---

This decree is one that I think is best displayed in the life of a child, particularly from the new birth to toddler stage of development. There is something fascinating about watching a child who has made it's way into the world, and is going through the process of discovery. When observing a child during these stages, you will notice that they have an interest to explore and touch everything that is in sight. Their level of curiosity is like no other. They carry this desire to connect with this new world, and search out it's meaning and inner details. Not only are they curious about the things that appear great, but for a child, a simple tugging at an earring and having the experience of tangibly grasping it is fulfilling to them (though not a great experience for the individual who's ear is connected to the earring). It is this same curiosity and childlike wonder that causes us to search out the things of God. This world is limited in what it's able to produce, but the things of the spirit have no end. God has no expiration date, and we never exhaust in finding out new things about Him. Our Daddy just keeps on giving. It's amazing to know that He is intentionally involved with each and every one of us and His relationship is unique towards each of us. He knows us best and loves us most. This relationship of discovery is full of adventure and mysteries. It could be described as playful in nature. In the process of searching out the things of God, you find that He has hidden all of these wonderful treasures for you. He has purposefully places "goodies" in specific places to be found by you! These treasures not only bless you, but they bless those around you. How could one ever get bored on this journey? If you're bored, it's because you stopped playing! We rest in Him as sons, but we never stop pursuing His heart. We never cease in our pursuit of discovering new depths of who He is. There are mysteries and secrets that have yet to be discovered and exposed to humanity. This is not because He is holding out on us, but He hides these things for us. There are times that the enemy would like to convince us that God is holding out on us, as he did with Eve in the garden. This couldn't be further from the Truth. This is seen when the Father sends what is most precious to Him, His Son, Jesus Christ, to die for all of humanity. He gave us His all in the Son and has freely made available to us all of heaven's mysteries. If He was willing to send His only begotten Son for you, who were once an enemy, imagine what He has hidden for you as a son!

# Decree #24

# "Walk by Faith"

*"... I live by faith in the Son of God ..."*

*–Gal. 2:20*

---

"…I live by faith in the Son…" Wait Paul, do you mean that I don't live by faith in my strength? Are you saying that faith isn't as gut wrenching as it sounds? That's exactly what I'm saying. Someone reading this is thinking, "Well you have to experience great hardship before you have faith," or "You don't know what I've been through to attain the level of faith that I have." I want to present a question to you, "What was your faith in the moment you received Jesus Christ as your Lord and Savior." When we receive Jesus as Savior, our faith is not centered in what we have experienced, rather it was based upon what He has done. Faith in its purest form is founded upon His works not ours. If we follow Paul's example, we never find him boasting in all that he has done to attain a certain level of faith. He keeps his gaze upon and glorifies the Son. Any time our faith is driven by anything else but the Son, it has the potential to fail us. It's all about Jesus!

Jesus modeled for us what the walk of faith looks like and how to ensure that it is efficient and effective in our life. The faith of the Son was in the Father. Jesus' faith, though He was God, was not in Himself. He came in the likeness of man, yet lived full of faith. I believe His faith was a direct result of the revelation He had of the Father. Jesus lived a life of constant communion with the Father. His every decision was done with the Father's heart in mind. His life displayed what it looked like to walk in a love relationship with God, and I believe that it was this revelation of love that empowered Him to walk in faith. Faith works through love. Jesus lived with His eyes gazed upon love (The Father). This is the model that we are to follow as sons and daughters. Paul reveals this to us in the statement, "I live by faith in the Son of God." The faith of Paul was in what Christ has done. His faith was in the perfection of the finished works of Jesus. His faith wasn't based upon the intensity of a situation, but it was based upon the furious love of Christ that was poured out upon the Cross. It was in the victorious resurrection of Jesus. In other words, His faith was a Person. While people have sought with good intentions to calculate the perfect formulas for faith development; the best way to put faith is simple, "Faith = Jesus." When our faith is in the Son, it is in perfection. When our faith is in His work, it allows us to rest, and with a sound mind, we are able to demonstrate the authority that God has given to us. This removes the pressure of performance, and allows you to walk with confidence in Him, and to manifest your natural identity as a child of God. Be encouraged to leverage this truth in your life, and to completely trust, rely, and rest in His finished work!

# Decree #25

# "If I had 10,000 tongues, they still wouldn't be enough to tell just how great He is!"

*"... His greatness is unsearchable ..."*

*–Psalms 145:3*

---

So often we have said or heard the statement, "God is good." The truth of this statement extends into dimensions that we will spend eternity discovering. The goodness of God reigns in a lane of it's own. His goodness is completely pure and incorruptible. As we continue to walk with Him, we find ourselves walking into new revelations of His goodness. Just when we think we can explain His goodness, He invites us into another part of Himself that simply leaves us speechless. It is this very goodness that takes your breath away when you discover that His love towards you is perfect and without change. It is this revelation that overwhelms the heart of man, and fills him with a holy awe for the person of Jesus Christ.

David said, "His greatness is unsearchable." The interpretation that I have received concerning that declaration is that I can "press" into God without ceasing, yet never exhaust His goodness. There's always more. So often, we feel as though we have hit the ceiling as it pertains to the measure of His goodness we can experience. My friends, I've got good news; You can have as much as you want. The Father has given you the fullness in the person of Jesus, yet there is this everlasting discovery that we have the privilege of experiencing with Him. So many feel as though they are not good enough or "qualified" to experience the more of God. There's more news; You don't and cannot quality yourself. Christ has qualified you and His blood has signed for you the certificate of qualification. He has not only qualified you, but He has invited you to partake of His goodness. It is not your perfect behavior that makes you candidate. It's the truth that you are His child, He loves you, and that His goodness towards you is not dependant upon your goodness towards Him. He is not waiting for you to mess up so that He can zap you. He doesn't disown you because you were naughty, He convicts you of righteousness (your identity), and restores you to honor. It is this goodness that offends the carnal mind, because it just doesn't make any sense. Who sends His only Son to die for His enemies? The Father. Who is He who hangs on a Cross and endures excruciating pain for a group of people who relentlessly mocks Him, spats on Him, and dishonors Him? The Son. Who has come to live within us in sweet communion and to walk with us in every moment? The Holy Spirit. Throughout His-story we find that His love and goodness towards man has always existed in a way that man alone couldn't understand. Yet it is this goodness that grips our heart and yells within our souls, "God loves you." Go forth with confidence knowing that you are loved, and that His goodness towards you is never-ending!

# Decree #26
# "You've been designed for the dream. "

*"Being confident of this very thing, that He who has begun a good work in you will complete it until the day of Jesus Christ"*
*Phil. 1:6*

---

Did you know that before you ever existed in time that you first existed in the heart of The Father? He ordained you to fulfill destiny before you ever knew what your purpose was. So often we forfeit our dreams and passions because we feel as though they are impossible or because we feel as though we aren't capable. These are nothing more than lies that the enemy uses to fight against our destiny and to undermine our fulfillment. Many have accepted these lies as truth, which has caused them to settle into lifestyles that are beneath what they were created to live. My friends, He would never tease you with a dream and inspire you with a passion that He wouldn't use. Who do you think inspired the dream? He has placed something within all of us to which we can use to positively impact the world. Someone is waiting on your dream. Someone is waiting on that vision. There is someone waiting to be encouraged by your CD and empowered by your book. I want to encourage you to never underestimate the gifts He has given you. What you have is of great significance and value.

Before going any further, I want you to grab a pen and paper. No seriously, grab a pen and paper. Now that you have those, I want you to take a moment to relax and close your eyes to imagine the life you would love to live. What does it look like? What are you doing? Who are you serving? What system are you impacting? Ready. Set. Go! Now I want you to take a moment and write those things down. If you could spend your life doing one thing what would it be? Now that you have written those things down, it is time to move beyond where most people stop. So often we write out a vision only to place it in a nice folder and let it collect dust. Now that you have your dreams on paper, I want you to grab another piece of paper. On the top of this sheet of paper I want you to write in big letters, "It Shall Come to Pass!!!" Under that I want you to write the dream. Now that we have declared it shall come to pass, the next order of business is how.

Now I want you to take a moment to pray and simply say,

*"Father, I thank You for the dream that You have planted within my heart. I thank You that it is of great significance. I thank You that You didn't just put it in me to stay there, but that You placed it within me to get it out. Now that I have acknowledged this, I come asking You for ideas, strategies, and initiatives to bring it forth. The spirit of wisdom and revelation be upon me and cause creativity to flow. I thank you that this dream shall not be miscarried nor shall it be aborted. I decree and declare that it shall come to pass! In Jesus name I pray. Amen"*

Now that you have prayed, rest in this truth, "You are His sheep and you hear His voice." Now take a few moments to write the ideas that come to mind (at least ten minutes). Now that you have written these ideas down you, have a responsibility to steward them. So often we lose hope of ever fulfilling the dreams He has placed in us because we see the big picture. We forget that more often than not, there is a road that leads to the manifestation of the big picture. It's called the process. On that road our only responsibilities are to fellowship with Holy Spirit and to be good stewards of what He gives us. You will never move beyond where you are if you never move! What can you do today to jump start you towards fulfilling what He has placed in your heart? It could be something as simple as starting a blog, practicing an instrument, applying for college, or buying a camera. You've been designed for this! The world is waiting on you! Heaven is backing you up and Papa is cheering you on! Go forth!

# Decree #27
# "What He reveals to you is yours. "

*"The secret things belong to the Lord our God, but the things which He revealed belong us..."*
*Duet. 29:29*

*"[For I always pray to the God of our Lord Jesus Christ, the Father of glory, that He may grant you a spirit of wisdom and revelation [of insight into mysteries and secrets] in the [deep and intimate] knowledge of Him"*
*Eph. 1:17*

---

Did you know that there are secrets and mysteries that God wants to share with you? So often we become settled in what we know about God and lose the innocence of discovery. When we examine the life of a child, we learn the key of revelation. Someone is saying, "Oh Lord, not another key!" Here goes, it's really simple. They're children!!! They're not settled in their ways nor are they aware of and know the meaning to everything around them. As you observe them, you will see that they take great joy in the process of discovery. They possess this innocence that causes them to have joy upon discovering the simplest thing. So often in the process of maturing we lose that childlike sense of discovery. We lose that awe that once caused us to leap and dance. Beloved, must we never forget that we too are children. We must never forget that God is our Father and that He takes delight in running with us through the fields of discovery and adventure. We will never run out of things to discover about God. He is beyond being totally figured out. Isn't that beautiful! We get to journey with Holy Spirit into the deeper things of God.

Along the road of discovery, He gives us treasures. These treasures that He gives us are called revelation. He entrusts us with these precious jewels. He doesn't gift us with revelation for it to collect dust on some shelf. These treasures are given to us to steward and apply within our lives. We have the great opportunity of sharing what He has given us with others. When we hold on to everything we are given, we tend to run out of space for other things. These treasures are all expressions of God's love, and love gives. Freely we receive as children and freely we are to give.

Holy Spirit reveals to us the deep things of God (1 Cor. 2:10) to mature us in the knowledge of Jesus Christ. All revelation that is inspired by God does two things. It reveals Christ and it glorifies Him before men. It reveals a different element of His goodness that wasn't previously realized. As the secrets of God are unveiled to us, it unveils us. The journey of self-discovery is revealed in Christ discovery. As we grow in the knowledge of Him, we grow in the knowledge of who we have been created to be. Infinite wisdom is found in the Person of Jesus Christ. This wisdom not only reveals Him, but it becomes a roadmap for us on the road to destiny. I want to challenge you to take the things He reveals to you and step into them. The revelation of the word becomes flesh as we dare to step into them. It's your birthright as a child of God to walk in the supernatural revelation of the Father. Remember this, "What He reveals to you is yours!"

# Decree #28

# "The fulfillment of your prophetic destiny awaits your "Yes!""

*"Submit yourselves to the Lord, and He will lift you up"*

*James 4:7*

---

Before we were birthed into time, the Father marked us to fulfill something specific in the earth. The pure reality of what we have been called to do is realized when we are born again into the Family of God. He reveals in our hearts what we He has called us to do and gives us directives for how to bring it forth. When people come into this revelation, there is an array of possible responses that occur. Some reject what they are shown because of how they view themselves, while others are afraid to move beyond where they are. So often, we allow our past to imprison our future. The spirit of fear is used as a weapon to abort what He has placed within us to birth. More often than not, people live by fear because they feel unqualified for the calling to which He has given them. My friends, I've got good news. God has furnished you with all things pertaining to life and godliness. He has instilled within you the grace to fulfill the call. The only thing He requires from you is your "Yes." In this age, we are so dependent upon logic that it tends create conflict around our ability to say yes. The truth is, "yes" doesn't mean that you understand everything. More often than not, you won't be able to dissect His initiatives with the logical mind. We walk by faith. Faith is completely illogical when it comes to the way this world functions. While we might not have all the pieces, there is assurance in the truth that our Father loves us and would never instruct us to do something that He wouldn't enable us to complete.

Our ability to complete rests in our willingness to submit. Someone is saying, "That doesn't sound like Grace." The truth is, the measure to which we are willing to say "Yes," is the measure to which we are willing to serve. So often, we fail to obey because we think we know what's best. Saul was given specific instructions from God, yet he felt that he knew what was best. This sabotaged his own position and caused him to miscarry his position of leadership. Where there is disobedience, there is un-fulfillment. He leads us intentionally. He knows all things, therefore He knows what is best for us. Our ability to say "Yes" to God increases as we grow in the revelation of His love for us. We are His children, and we have the best Dad. There is no good parent that would intentionally lead their children into a place to purposely harm them. Beloved, you are in the best hands!

I want to challenge you to examine your life and the initiatives that the Father has placed within your heart that have been ignored. The awesome thing about Him is that He enables you to redeem the time. The truth is, you never know who and what could possibly be connected to your "Yes." It could be something as simple as going down aisle seven at Wal-Mart (inside joke for a special reader) to pray for someone, or something as great as starting your own business. Imagine the potential effect that your yes could have in history. Jesus' "Yes" is impacting us over two thousand years later, and will continue to impact heaven throughout all eternity. Never underestimate the power of surrender. Now right there where you are, tell God "Yes!"

# Decree #29

# "Sin is out.
# Righteousness is in."

*"For sin shall not have dominion over you, for you are not under law but under grace.*

*Romans 6:14*

---

Sin is so outdated. It was defeated by Righteousness Himself over 2,000 years ago. In the person of Jesus Christ, we have been given total dominion over everything that this nature represents. It once ruled us and was enticed by the Law, but Christ has cancelled out the law, disarming the very weapon that principalities and powers used against us. Over here in grace, it's a whole new world.

I've got a news flash my friends! You are no longer identified as sinners. You are identified as sons and daughter. There are many that would seek to mix Law and Grace, but they are completely different. Under Law, man was dependant upon how well they could perform to keep the "written code." The truth is, no one could keep it. If you broke one law, you broke the entire list of written rules. God didn't initiate the Law, the children of Israel did. In pride, they told Moses to go and get a list of rules from God to follow and that they would keep them. They didn't want relationship with God; they simply wanted rules. This resembles how much of today's church functions. Though God is displaying His power and love towards man, they seem to ignore His invitation to union, and gravitate towards performing for acceptance. This was an impossible task for man to fulfill. God never desired to bind man with the law. The Law is for the unrighteous. Christ came and perfectly fulfilled the Law, thus making those who would accept Him as Lord, the righteousness of God in Christ. Beloved we are justified (made righteous, made to have right standing) by faith. This faith is not in our ability to perfectly maintain a list of rules. It's in the ability of Christ, what He accomplished on the Cross, and who He has made us to be.

Proper belief precedes proper manifestation. It is so imperative that our belief be inspired by truth. So often the Law sounds so much more believable because it means we have to do all of the work. It means that we get to boast in how sanctified, saved, and holy we are.

The truth is, if you can boast about those things, you have not entered into the Grace of God. Over here in Grace, our boast is in the Lord, His work, His sanctification, His righteousness, and all that He has done. Now I am not saying that Grace is a license to sin, nor am I saying that it gives you permission to do whatever. What I am saying is that by God's grace, which has been poured out in the Person of Jesus Christ, you can rest in your identity as the righteous. Your old man has been buried and you have been brought forth by the glory of the Father to walk in this new identity. You are no longer a slave to sin's beckon and call. If you are in Christ, that old man is outdated. Leave that old fad in the grave and embrace the garment that has come as a free gift by the Son.

# Decree #30

## "The Glory is the full expression of God, who He is, and what He has. His children have access to this reality."

*"For through Him we both have access by one Spirit to the Father"*

*Eph. 2:18*

---

Wouldn't it seem appropriate that all glory belongs to God, being that He is Glory. The Glory is a Person. It is the full expression of all that God is and all that He has. Glory goes far beyond a good word to shout in the middle of a church service. When this reality is realized, you find the solution to every problem and the answer to every question that has been long standing in your life. The Father is the source from which all things have come to be. This being true, it makes perfect since that every need has been met according to the riches in "glory." Riches represent everything that pertains to life and godliness. He has granted His children full access in the heavenly realm to every spiritual and natural blessing. It is our birthright as the family of God to walk in this reality.

Jesus died so to bring us into the glory (Heb. 2:10). We have co-ascended with Him and in this present time we are seated in the heavenly realm in Christ. This truth when grasped changes the position from which we perceive life. It changes the position from which we function and communicate with God. Instead of begging in prayer, we are empowered to decree a thing and see it established. We can so this as sons and daughters because we have access to the Father. It is His pleasure to give us the kingdom by manifesting Himself through us in the world.

Would you like to know how we enter into this reality? We do so by faith. This is done by taking hold of this truth, declaring it, and stepping out to make a demand on it. Worship is another way we enter into this reality. Around the throne of the Father in the glory, worship occurs continually. Worship awakens the reality

of the glory that continually exists around us.
Have you ever noticed how light the atmosphere
becomes around you when you begin to worship
God? It is because you are emulating what is
currently taking place in heaven, thus it
increases your sensitivity to that realm. You
were originally birthed out of, and have been re-
created for the Glory. It's home. Jesus died to
remove the distance between you and the Glory
that was created by the sin of the first Adam.
Awaken to the reality of the Glory, where He
works, and you rest. It's like heaven on earth!

# Decree #31

# "I've given you the Best Friend on earth. Me."

*"The grace (favor and spiritual blessing) of the Lord Jesus Christ and the love of God and the presence and fellowship (the communion and sharing together, and participation) in the Holy Spirit be with you all. Amen (so be it)."*

## *2 Cor. 13:14*

---

The Spirit of God, the Comforter, and the Spirit of glory are just a few names to describe the precious Holy Spirit. Jesus went away, yet we weren't left alone. The Father sent us a friend on earth that we can count on to be there and never leave. He sent us Himself in the Person of the Holy Spirit. The One who formed the universe, heals sick bodies, and quickened Christ's mortal body to be raised form the dead. It is He that we have the great privilege of having fellowship and friendship with. So often, we limit Him to the chills we feel in worship, or the "it" that magically enters the sanctuary on a Sunday morning. The truth is, that He is always with us.

Holy Spirit is just as much God as the Father and Son. The truth that the Father sent Himself to not only dwell with, but to live in us is mind blowing. He is the treasure that the Father has placed in earthen vessels. God Himself has taken residence within us. This is sure proof that God values His relationship with mankind. It wasn't enough to send Jesus to die for us, He desired that all distance be removed. David asked a question, "What is man that You are mindful of him?" My friends, if you've ever questioned the degree to which God loves and values you think about this, "God chose you to be the place on earth in which He would reside." That alone is a mystery that should produce awe in the hearts of humanity.

We have been invited into this beautiful journey with Him. He desires to be our best friend here on earth. Did you know that He desires to be involved in your life beyond the walls of the church building? He desires to be involved in your life just as much when you're washing dishes as when you're praying for people. He's there during the best of times as well as the worst of times. He wants to laugh with you, and hold you when you're crying. He wants to empower you to minister to the hopeless as well as inspiring the way you lead your family. It's through intimacy with the Holy Spirit that you grow in the revelation of the Father and your identity in Him. It is through this close relationship, that He wants to use you to change the world. Cultivating a relationship of intimacy with the Holy Spirit enables you to live with a greater awareness of Him. It awakens your being to the very overshadowing and indwelling power of God. As you grow in relationship with the Holy Spirit, you become sensitive to the heart of the Father. As a result, you are enabled to live and love freely.

The revelation that comes through intimacy with the Holy Spirit doesn't come simply by reading the Scriptures. Jesus told the Pharisees that they thought by searching out the scriptures alone that they would inherit eternal life, but that what He truly desired was for them to come to Him. Eternal life is knowing God. He is the Scripture. The Holy Spirit is the revealer of the deep things of God. He escorts us into the mysteries of the kingdom that we could never encounter on our own. He not only reveals to us the deep mysteries hidden in the written word, but He also reveals the destiny written in our hearts. He is a lamp unto our feet, leading us into the truth of who we have been created to be. He has been sent as a Friend to whom we can rest in as we journey throughout our lives. Embrace the beauty of this relationship, Beloved. Forsake not the fellowship of the Holy Spirit.

# Prayer

---

The following prayer is to seal what you've experienced as you read this book. It is my personal prayer that your life has been impacted by the truth revealed in Jesus Christ. Never again settle for a life that is beneath the life Christ died for you to live.

*Father, I thank you for Jesus. I thank you for His coming, dying, and resurrection. It is in Him that I am complete and made whole. I thank you that in Him I have been grafted into the family of God and am no longer an orphan. I receive His finished work on the Cross. I believe in His complete work and from a position of resting in Him; I manifest His finished work. I declare that my mind wont be deceived nor will my heart be convinced of anything but truth. This truth is that You radically and relentlessly love me, and You value for my is seen in that You sent Your only begotten Son to die for me. This is the dawning of a new day and I go forth as a new creation in Christ. Thank you Father for this great identity that you have given me. With the revelation that*

*I have received I am empowered to live freely and love freely. I declare and decree that my life is forever established, grounded, and rooted in love. In Jesus' name, Amen.*

This next prayer is for those who have read and want to receive salvation and the baptism of the Holy Spirit. He loves you so much and sent Christ to restore broken relationship between you and Him.

*Father, I thank you for sending Jesus to reconcile us. I believe that He is Your only begotten Son, and that He died on a Cross, was buried, and rose again. He was the beautiful exchange. I receive the love you have freely extended to me in Christ and I give my life to you. I receive the salvation of Christ, and proclaim that He is my Lord and Savior. I also ask for the baptism of the Holy Spirit that is freely given to those who ask for it. I receive it as a gift. I also ask for the gift of my supernatural language. Thank you for the precious gift of the Holy Spirit. Thank you for saving and filling me. I receive in Jesus' name. Amen!*

# Appendix

*The following is a list of Scriptures and declarations that further reveal, confirm, and affirm your identity in Christ. Meditate on them, declare them, and walk therein.*

I am loved. (John 3:16)

I am forgiven. (1 John 1:9)

I am a new creation in Christ. This me has never existed before. (2 Cor. 5:21)

I'm a child and I have access to the Father through the Holy Spirit. (Eph. 2:18)

I am a saint. (Eph. 1:1)

I am royalty. (1 Pet. 2:9)

I have authority over the power of the devil. (Luke 10:19)

I am taught by grace. (Titus 2:12)

I'm anointed to run and to finish. (2 Tim. 4:7)

I was made to look like my Daddy. (Gen 1:27)

I have been co-crucified, co-buried, and co-risen with Christ. (Rom. 6)

I have dominion over sin. (Rom. 6:14)

I have the mind of Christ. (1 Cor. 2:16)

I am complete in Christ. (Col. 2:10)

Christ in me is the hope of Glory. (Col. 1:27)

I am redeemed. (Rom 3:24)

I am sanctified. (1 Cor. 6:15)

I am the righteousness of God in Christ. (2 Cor. 5:21)

Christ is my garment. I wear Him everywhere that I go. (Gal. 3:27)

I am seated with Christ in the heavenly realm. (Eph. 2:6)

I am blessed with all spiritual blessings in the heavenly realm. (Eph. 1:3)

I have boldness in Christ. (Eph. 3:12)

I am redeemed from the curse of the law. (Gal. 3:13)

I have the spirit of power, love and a sound mind. Fear has no rights in my life. (2 Tim. 1:7)

I am healed. Sickness was defeated in the Body of Christ. I have perfect health. I am whole. (Isa. 53:5)

I am rooted and grounded in love. (Eph 3:17)

His spirit of might strengthens me and energizes me with supernatural power. (Eph. 3:16)

I am daily loaded with benefits. (Ps. 68:19)

The blessing of the Lord makes me rich and is free of sorrow. (Prov 10:22)

Goodness and mercy follows me everyday. (Ps. 23:6)

My head is anointed with oil; my cup overflows. (Ps. 23:5)

Christ has brought me into the glory. (Heb 2:10)

I rest in Christ. (Heb. 4:9-10)

The spirit of wisdom and revelation rests upon me. (Eph. 17)

I am the fragrance of Christ. (2 Cor. 2:14)

As He is, so am I in the world. (1 John 4:17)

I am holy and blameless. (Eph. 1:4)

God is for me. (Rom. 8:31)

I have right standing with God. (Rom. 8:33)

My life is hidden in Christ. (Col. 3:3)

I am a citizen of heaven. (Phil. 3:20)

My joy is full. (1 John 1:4)

I share in His divine nature. (2 Pet. 1:4)

I have resurrection power on the inside of me. (Rom. 8:11)

I overcome by His blood and the word of my testimony. (Rev. 12:11)

# About The Author

**KeVon Pippens** is the founder of Kingdom Pioneers Ministries. He along with his wife, Cedrica Pippens, currently resides in Murfreesboro, TN. He has a passion to see the Body of Christ live in the reality of their true identity in Christ and to see the lost reconciled back to Christ. His heart is to see the world reformed through the power of the gospel of the Kingdom.

For more information visit
**www.KPMNOW.com**